Dua Lipa Biography:

The Untold Story of a Global Pop
Sensation – How a Fearless Singer
Redefined Music, Fashion, and Pop
Culture.

Caroline A. Minter

Dua Lipa

Disclaimer:

The following book is for entertainment and informational purposes only.The stories, events, and dialogue recreated in this biography are based on extensive research, interviews, and the author's own interpretation of the available information.

Dua Lipa

Table of Contents

Dua Lipa

Who is Dua Lipa?

One of the most well-known music stars in the world right now is Dua Lipa. She is well-known for her distinctive fashion sense, powerful voice, and catchy tunes. But she was only a young woman with a tremendous dream before she rose to fame. On August 22, 1995, Dua Lipa was born in London, England. Her parents hailed from the tiny European nation of Kosovo. In an attempt to improve their lot in life, they relocated to London before her birth. Dua was raised in a musical household. She grew up hearing a variety of musical genres at home, thanks to her father, Dukagjin Lipa, who was also a musician. She was greatly impacted by this, which deepened her music appreciation.

Dua Lipa

Dua was self-assured and enjoyed performing as a child. She would perform small shows for her family and sing around the house. When she was just five years old, she began singing along to songs by well-known performers like Christina Aguilera and Nelly Furtado. Her parents encouraged her to continue practicing after noticing her enthusiasm. She furthered her education in music and performance at London's Sylvia Young Theatre School.

Dua's family, however, made the decision to return to Kosovo when she was eleven years old. For her, this was a significant shift. Adapting to a new culture, forming new friendships, and learning a new way of life were all part of moving to a new nation. She missed London and its prospects, but she adored spending time with her

Dua Lipa

family. She was aware that she had to return to her most promising place if she wished to pursue a career as a singer.

Dua, who was fifteen at the time, took a risk. In order to pursue music, she persuaded her parents to allow her to return to London alone. For someone so young, it was a major risk, but she had confidence in herself. She took her studies seriously, moved in with a family friend, and put a lot of effort into realizing her goals. She worked as a waitress and a model since she had to support herself, but music was always her genuine love.

Dua began recording and posting cover songs to YouTube. In the hopes that someone in the music business would recognize her skills, she performed songs by singers she liked. Social media was

Dua Lipa

beginning to alter how individuals got famous at the time, and Dua saw this as her chance. She had a distinctive voice that was strong, emotional, and deep. Her films quickly began receiving more and more attention.

More and more people found her as she continued to share her songs online. Music producers eventually began contacting her. She had a chance one day that would forever alter her life. She was offered a deal by a record label when they recognized her skills. Dua was incredulous. She was finally having the opportunity to pursue a career in music after years of arduous effort.

Her career really took off after she released her first single in 2015. Because her music was new, up-to-date, and energetic, people

Dua Lipa

adored it. "New Rules," one of her greatest hits, went viral all over the world. With its message of self-assurance and letting go of toxic relationships, the song resonated with millions of listeners worldwide. Not only did the song have an impact, but the music video, which featured strong female backing, was equally imaginative and potent. Dua became even more well-liked as a result, particularly with young girls who viewed her as an inspiration.

In addition to creating music, Dua Lipa was revolutionizing the field. People adored the lively dance-pop sound she revived, and she didn't hesitate to try out new looks. With tracks that made people want to dance, her second album, "Future Nostalgia," became an enormous success. Her songs made

Dua Lipa

people happy all around the world, even in trying times like the COVID-19 pandemic.

Dua became a fashion icon in addition to being a musician. She visited important fashion events, collaborated with well-known designers, and even launched her own brand. She always had a strong, vibrant, and distinctive style. She demonstrated the benefits of standing out and being unique. In addition to her music, she was admired by many young people for her self-assurance and uniqueness.

The success of Dua Lipa extended beyond her career in fashion and music. She also raised awareness of significant topics by using her platform. She has been a fervent advocate for mental health awareness, women's rights, and aiding refugees. She frequently discusses how her own

Dua Lipa

family had to flee their homeland in search of a better life, and she is motivated to support those facing comparable challenges.

She has received numerous accolades throughout the years, including several Grammys and Brit Awards. Every honor served as a reminder of her progress when she was a little kid, posting videos to YouTube. However, she maintains her modesty and dedication to her love of music in spite of all the recognition and success.

Dua Lipa is a worldwide superstar now, not just a singer. Her story demonstrates that with perseverance, hard effort, and self-belief, aspirations may come true. She took chances, had modest beginnings, and never gave up. She continues to inspire

Dua Lipa

millions of people worldwide, whether it be through her activism, clothes, or music. She also demonstrates her permanence with every new song and endeavor, influencing pop music for years to come.

Dua Lipa

Chapter 1: Beginnings and Influences

August 22, 1995, saw the birth of Dua Lipa in London, England. She was raised surrounded by music, love, and the rich cultural customs of her family. Her parents, Anesa Lipa and Dukagjin Lipa, were originally from the small southeastern European nation of Kosovo. Before she was born, they relocated to London hoping to start a new life. They brought their customs and music passion with them despite leaving their native country. Dua's father used to play the tunes she grew up listening to. Being a musician himself, his love of music permeated their house. This greatly impacted her and changed how she perceived the world.

Dua had a large personality and a powerful voice from an early age. She enjoyed attempting to match every note precisely as she sang along to the music she heard on the radio. Her parents pushed her to continue singing after spotting her potential early on. She took in every melody and lyric as they frequently played music by well-known performers like Stereophonics, Bob Dylan, and David Bowie. She also kept in touch with her heritage by listening to Albanian music.

Dua has confidence in herself even as a young child. She never shied away from performing in front of an audience. She would sing whenever she had the opportunity, whether at home, school, or family get-togethers. She knew deep down that singing was what she wanted to do for

Dua Lipa

the rest of her life since it made her feel the happiest.

When she was just five years old, she began to take music more seriously. She enrolled at London's renowned performing arts school, the Sylvia Young Theatre School. Here, she developed confidence in addition to learning more about singing and performing. Being surrounded by young people who shared her passion for music encouraged her to keep getting better. But when she was eleven years old, her life changed drastically.

Her family made the decision to return to Kosovo that year. They decided to raise Dua and her brothers in their native country, even though it was a tough choice for them. This was both thrilling and frightening for Dua. Having only made a few previous

Dua Lipa

trips to Kosovo, she now had to get used to a whole different way of life. The language, the culture, and even the style of life were all different. She never gave up on her dream of being a singer despite the fact that she missed London.

Dua found herself looking for methods to maintain her musical connection while she was in Kosovo. She composed lyrics in her notebook, sang whenever she could, and listened to her favorite musicians. However, she also understood that she needed to be in London if she wanted to succeed in the music business. She frequently shared her desire to become a singer with her parents, who encouraged her but acknowledged that it wouldn't be simple.

Dua made one of the most audacious choices of her life when she was

Dua Lipa

fifteen. She was able to persuade her parents to allow her to return to London independently. She was aware that her best opportunity to take music seriously would be in the city. Because of their faith in her, her parents let her reside with a family friend while she pursued her studies. Despite the significant risk, Dua was adamant about demonstrating her readiness.

It was difficult to move to London by yourself. She needed to look after herself, attend school, and figure out how to finance her dream. She performed some modeling and worked as a waiter in restaurants to earn money. But music was always her primary concern. In the hopes that someone in the business would take notice, she began recording cover songs and posting them to YouTube. She added

Dua Lipa

her own special touch to covers of songs by musicians such as Christina Aguilera and Alicia Keys.

Her stage was the internet. She wanted to capitalize on the way social media was transforming the discovery of new musicians. Her videos began to garner notice gradually. Her voice was deep, strong, and emotional, and people adored it. She stood out from other vocalists because of the way she sounded.

With each video that Dua posted, her confidence increased. She was writing her own songs in addition to performing others'. She created music that felt authentic by drawing on her own thoughts, feelings, and experiences. She wanted her songs to have a deeper impact on listeners and felt that music should tell a story.

Dua Lipa

Music producers eventually became aware of her talent. They wanted to help her improve her sound since they thought she had a unique quality. She finally received the call she had been anticipating one day: a record deal offer. Though she knew it was only the beginning, it was a dream come true. This was the beginning of the actual labor.

Dua's work was greatly influenced by her early experiences. She learned important lessons from traveling between two different countries, taking a significant risk at the age of 15, and growing up in a musical environment. She discovered the value of self-belief, perseverance, and hard work. She accepted rather than concealed the fact that she was special because of her heritage.

Dua Lipa

Her roots got ingrained in her music rather than merely existing in her history. She performed with the self-assurance she had as a child. Her songwriting reflected the complex customs of her Albanian background. Every obstacle she encountered served as inspiration for her to keep going.

In retrospect, it is evident that all of her experiences contributed to her success. She got to where she is now by taking tiny steps like singing in her living room, going to music school, relocating to Kosovo, and posting covers on YouTube. Dreams do not come true overnight, as her experience demonstrates. They require a great deal of guts, time, and work.

Dua Lipa would go on to become one of the most significant pop stars in the world,

Dua Lipa

shatter records, and collect accolades as her journey progressed. At her core, though, she remained the same young woman who had previously performed in front of her family in the hopes that the world would eventually hear her voice.

Dua Lipa

Chapter 2: Digital Dreams – From YouTube to Mainstream

Dua Lipa's path to success was unconventional unlike many performers who came before her. To become a well-known vocalist in the past, one typically had to perform at small events, get noticed by a record label, or compete in music competitions. However, Dua entered the music business at a moment of transition. She sensed an opportunity when young artists found new opportunities on the internet. Instead of waiting for a record label to discover her, she put herself out there.

Dua had always had a deep love for music as a child. Her voice was distinctively deep and soulful, and she enjoyed listening to various singers. However, having talent was insufficient. She required a means of being heard. She resorted to the internet at that point. Social media was expanding quickly, and sites like YouTube were allowing people to show off their abilities to a worldwide audience. This may be her ticket in, Dua realized.

She began recording and posting her renditions of well-known songs to YouTube when she was barely fourteen years old. She picked music by artists she liked, such as Christina Aguilera, Pink, and Nelly Furtado, and they weren't just any tunes. She sang them in a different style than the original performers. She gave them a personal touch by using her distinctive, deep voice and distinctive manner. With every video she shared, she had the

Dua Lipa

opportunity to expand her audience and demonstrate her abilities.

Few people first recognized her. She began modestly, like many YouTube singers who aspire to be famous. However, that didn't deter her. She continued to publish, continued to get better, and—above all—remained reliable. Her videos gradually began to receive more views. This young girl with a strong voice started to draw attention. Some people complimented her talent in their comments. Her movies were shared by others, expanding her audience. Even without a record deal, she was gaining a following.

Dua's ability to connect with people was one of the factors contributing to the growth of her internet presence. She wasn't merely posting videos and crossing her fingers. She

Dua Lipa

interacted with her audience. She allowed people to see her true self by responding to remarks and displaying her individuality. Because of this, she felt more like a friend than simply another vocalist and more relatable.

Her ascent to stardom was greatly aided by social media. Dua took advantage of the growing popularity of sites like SoundCloud, Instagram, and Twitter. She gave viewers a chance to relate to her personally by sharing tidbits of her life in addition to singing videos. People were attracted to her as a person in addition to her music. She was self-assured, fashionable, and genuine.

When record labels and music producers began to take notice of her online presence, it was one of the most significant turning points in her digital path. Industry

Dua Lipa

insiders were observing her in the same way that fans were learning about her. She stood out from the multitudes of other singers vying for attention thanks to her distinctive voice and rising fame. She was making an opportunity rather than waiting for one.

She was eventually approached by a manager who saw her potential. She had been waiting for this time. It had finally paid off after all the years she had spent publishing covers and interacting online. She started writing original music after signing a contract. But despite this fresh chance, she never lost sight of her beginnings. By providing behind-the-scenes photos and engaging her supporters in her journey, she persisted in using social media to develop her brand.

Dua Lipa

She benefited from her online presence in ways that were previously unattainable. Prior to the internet, musicians had to rely on television and radio stations to promote their music. However, Dua could share her music with millions of people online without waiting for someone to play it on the radio. Because of the fan base she had already established, her first few singles were well-received when they were released. People who had followed the artist from her YouTube days were thrilled to lend their support.

Her release of "New Rules" was one of her most significant moments. The way the song propagated online was more important than the music itself, even though it became an immediate smash. Within days, the imaginative and eye-catching music video

Dua Lipa

became viral. It was widely shared by fans, who produced reaction videos, dance covers, and memes. Her song had taken on a life of its own on social media. She was leveraging the digital world to take charge of her success rather than waiting for traditional media to make her famous.

The success of Dua demonstrates the potency of internet media. She was among the first to completely embrace the internet, which revolutionized the way artists interact with their fans. Before she ever had an album, she established herself by using Twitter, Instagram, and YouTube. She demonstrated that success could be attained with skill, diligence, and a strong internet presence.

Looking back on her path, it's evident that her rise to fame was greatly aided by the

Dua Lipa

internet. Today's young artists find inspiration in her narrative. She demonstrated that you don't need to wait for someone else to fulfill your dreams. You only need to use the tools that are already available.

She continued to draw on her digital roots as her career progressed. She continued to share her life and songs on social media, keeping in touch with her followers even after she became a worldwide phenomenon. Adopting digital innovation may transform a career, as demonstrated by her journey from YouTube covers to mainstream fame.

A significant lesson may be learned from Dua's story: the internet has altered the game, and people who use it responsibly can take advantage of chances that previously appeared unattainable. She

Dua Lipa

didn't begin with a well-known last name or contacts in the business. She began with a camera, a love of music, and self-confidence. She made her digital aspirations a reality by being persistent, imaginative, and involved.

Her success was a result of planning, tenacity, and an awareness of how the world was changing, not just good fortune. She was aware that social media was a tool and not only for enjoyment. She took advantage of it, demonstrating that success in the modern world requires more than simply talent; it also requires the ability to share that talent with the appropriate people.

Dua continues to be a shining example of how technology and music may coexist in the ever-evolving digital environment. By demonstrating that they don't need to wait

Dua Lipa

to be discovered, she paved the way for a new generation of artists. Like she did, they can forge their own route.

This is not the end of her adventure. She keeps using digital media to influence her career with every new song and endeavor. She is a living example of how talent and technology can work together to make dreams come true in the contemporary music industry. Her narrative serves as a lesson to young artists worldwide that everything is achievable if you're prepared to put yourself out there.

Dua Lipa

Chapter 3: The Breakout Hit – 'New Rules' and Rising Fame

Dua Lipa was a budding musician attempting to leave a lasting impression on the music business prior to "New Rules" being a worldwide success. Her fan base was constantly expanding, and she had published a couple of singles that garnered recognition. She still hadn't scored that one big hit, though, that would have advanced her career. She and her crew were working on their self-titled first album, trying to find the song that would best capture her as an artist.

When she heard "New Rules," she realized it was unique. The song stood out due to its distinctive structure, strong message, and catchy tempo. Many people might identify

Dua Lipa

with the song's message of self-respect and letting go of a destructive relationship. The song's lyrics spoke about strength, self-assurance, self-worth, and grief. The song made it easy to remember and relate by listing three "rules" to assist someone in avoiding an ex.

Not everyone first saw the song's potential, and not everyone in the music business was certain that it would be a huge success. Dua, however, felt strongly about it. She trusted that the song's message would resonate with listeners. She was aware that "New Rules" had the potential to be exceptional with the correct approach.

The song's production was as distinctive as its lyrics. The song used a unique blend of contemporary pop music and tropical house beats. The lyrics had a deeper

Dua Lipa

meaning, but the music had a captivating rhythm that made people want to dance. Not all pop songs are able to strike the ideal balance between enjoyment and emotional depth.

The music video for "New Rules" was a major turning point. Dua and her group understood that images were as vital as lyrics in the digital age. They desired an exceptional experience. They went with a strong and original idea rather than the usual music video love story or party scenario. In the footage, a group of women and Dua were shown in a hotel room, encouraging and physically restraining one another from making poor choices. It represented camaraderie, inner strength, and feminine empowerment.

Dua Lipa

The choreography in the video was captivating. It was visually remarkable because of the way the girls flowed together, almost like a human chain. Every element, including the color schemes and fluid motions, enhanced the video's allure. It was a statement rather than merely a music video. It sent a message that young people worldwide, particularly women, could relate to.

The video became viral as soon as it was made public. In a matter of days, it became popular on YouTube and had millions of views. People were discussing it, posting videos, and reenacting the dance on social media in droves. The song's theme of self-empowerment resonated with fans, and the music video strengthened their bond.

Dua Lipa

Industry insiders and music critics soon noticed. Dua Lipa was now a budding star rather than merely an up-and-coming talent. The song rose to the top of the charts, peaking at number one in the UK and breaking into the top ten in a number of other nations, including the US. It became her first number-one single, demonstrating that she was a real force in the business and not simply another pop singer.

The influence of "New Rules" extended beyond its radio exposure, setting it apart from many other pop singles. It turned into an anthem. Its lyrics were cited in the captions of social media posts. It was featured on playlists for workouts, at parties, and even at gatherings that encouraged independence and self-assurance. The

Dua Lipa

song was a cultural event rather than merely a piece of music.

Dua accepted her sudden notoriety with poise and resolve. She was aware of how "New Rules" had transformed her life, but she also realized that this was only the start. She wants to have a long-lasting career rather than become famous for a single song.

"New Rules" gave her the boost she needed to keep going. She sang the song on some of the biggest stages in the world, on award events, and on major TV shows. She became more confident with every performance. She developed her stage appearance and gained recognition for her vivacity and strong live singing.

She performed a beautiful rendition of the song with an all-female dance troupe at the

Dua Lipa

Brit Awards, which stands out as one of her most memorable performances. The show was daring and fashionable and encapsulated the song's spirit flawlessly. It was evident that Dua Lipa was a movement rather than merely a pop star.

The popularity of "New Rules" gave her access to opportunities she never would have thought possible. Magazines wanted her on their covers, brands wanted to work with her, and other artists wanted to cooperate with her. She immediately rose to fame as a fashion star because of her bold and edgy look. She made daring decisions that distinguished her from other artists, and designers flocked to clothe her.

She remained loyal to herself at the same time. She stayed grounded in spite of her quick ascent to celebrity. She frequently

Dua Lipa

talked about her experience, letting supporters know that it took time to achieve success. To get to where she was, she had to strive for years, endure rejection, and take chances.

In retrospect, "New Rules" marked a turning point in her career rather than merely a successful single. It was the song that made her widely known and demonstrated her permanence in the industry. It also demonstrated that extraordinary success may result from taking chances, having faith in your vision, and sticking with your innovative decisions.

Her digital roots were also linked to "New Rules" ' success. She had posted cover songs to YouTube years before in an attempt to gain attention. She was now producing music that was popular on the

Dua Lipa

same site. She had discovered how to take advantage of the internet, which had been a significant part of her path.

"New Rules," delivered by Dua Lipa. She wasn't going to stop there, though. One chapter came to a close with the song, and another began. She was already considering her next move, how to improve her voice and how to push her music to new heights.

She wanted to keep pushing limits, try new things, and take greater chances as she went. She wanted to transform the music business, contribute something new, and leave a lasting legacy since she wasn't content to be simply another pop star.

She then had to figure out how to win "New Rules." Would she be able to develop further as an artist? Could she make even

Dua Lipa

more impactful music? As she entered the next stage of her career, she was prepared to respond to these inquiries.

Dua Lipa

Chapter 4: Reinvention with Future Nostalgia

Dua Lipa knew that staying the same was never an option in the music business. Only those who dared to change with the times could survive in the fast-paced world of pop music. She had established herself as a formidable force following the success of her debut album. She desired more, though. Being another pop artist with a few hits wasn't what she wanted. Her goal was to produce something that would last and give them a sense of life. Her second studio album, *Future Nostalgia*, resulted from this desire and would not only revolutionize her career but also alter the pop music genre.

Dua had a vision before she began recording the album. She was looking for something new but familiar that would sound new but evoke nostalgia. She was captivated by the notion of fusing contemporary manufacturing with vintage inspirations. She realized there was something special about the disco, funk, and 80s pop music she had grown up listening to. They brought joy and made people dance. Her goal was to revive that spirit while adding a contemporary touch.

She collaborated with some of the top composers and producers in the business. Experiments took place in the studio every day. She didn't hesitate to push boundaries or take chances. She wanted the lyrics to be empowering, the melodies to be catchy, and the beats to be bold. Disco-inspired rhythms and powerful basslines were the foundation for songs like *Don't Start Now* and

Dua Lipa

Physical, but they also had a futuristic feel. Even when people were alone in their rooms, Dua wanted her music to inspire confidence and a desire to dance.

Recording Future Nostalgia required more than just writing catchy tunes. The goal was to create an experience. Dua considered every aspect, including the music and the images. She pictured people shouting along at the top of their lungs, dancing in their kitchens, or playing her tunes while driving down the highway. She envisioned this album as a universe unto itself, one that kept listeners firmly in the present while taking them to a distant era.

She had no idea what was going to happen when she released the record in 2020. The globe was experiencing an unanticipated catastrophe. Everything had changed

Dua Lipa

because of the COVID-19 epidemic. Concerned and unsure of what lay ahead, people were confined to their houses. Most musicians at the time would have postponed the release of their albums. Dua, however, took a different route. She thought that individuals could escape and feel better when they listened to music. She, therefore, chose to deliver *Future Nostalgia* at the precise moment when people needed it rather than waiting.

The record was an immediate hit. It was cheerful, vibrant, and full of life—everything that people had been missing. It was hailed by critics as one of the most daring pop albums in recent memory. Fans fell in love with it because it gave them hope for the future and brought back memories of better times. People who needed something to

Dua Lipa

cling to during trying times played songs like *Levitating* and *Break My Heart* repeatedly, turning them into anthems.

However, Future Nostalgia's popularity was due to more than just its music. It had to do with what it stood for. Dua has demonstrated that she was more than just a pop singer who followed fashion. They were being set by her. By abandoning the sound of her debut album, she had taken a chance, and it had paid off. She demonstrated to the world that she was here to stay by reinventing herself.

This was not an easy reinvention. She occasionally questioned whether others would embrace this new version of herself. But she followed her gut and pressed forth. She reflected on the great artists who had preceded her, the ones who had maintained

Dua Lipa

their relevance through perpetual change. Artists like Madonna, David Bowie, and Prince were never content with remaining in one spot for very long. They continued to evolve and surprise people. That's what made them legendary, and Dua wanted to be just that.

Future Nostalgia had an indisputable effect. It topped international charts, garnered several accolades, and solidified Dua's status as one of the most significant musicians of her generation. It altered the music business itself as well. Future Nostalgia revived the energy of dance music after years of slower, moodier pop dominated the charts. It demonstrated that reinvention might influence not only an artist's career but also an entire genre by encouraging other musicians to adopt retro sounds.

The success of the CD has equally amazing backstories. There were times in the studio when Dua and her crew realized they were working on something truly unique. There were also difficult times, such as when she had to persuade people that changing course was the best course of action. She never gave up, though. The difference was entirely due to her belief in the music.

When *Levitating* became one of the year's most popular songs, it was one of the most unforgettable moments. Once people heard the song, they couldn't stop listening to it, even though it nearly didn't make the album. The song has a timeless feel to it, effortlessly fusing contemporary pop with

Dua Lipa

70s funk. Dua's gamble paid off because it was so well received by fans that it became one of the longest-running songs on the Billboard charts.

The *Future Nostalgia* the tour produced another remarkable tale. The world was anxious to see live music when it eventually opened up again. Dua's tour was a celebration rather than merely a show. Fans wore daring costumes that were influenced by her fashion sense, joined in on dances, and sung along to every word as if it were their own. It served as a reminder of the importance of music and the ability of performers like Dua to unite people even under the most trying circumstances.

The main takeaway from *Future Nostalgia* was straightforward: longevity is mostly dependent on evolution. Dua might

Dua Lipa

have enjoyed short-term success if she had been cautious and stuck to what had previously worked. But that wasn't all she wanted. Her goal was to establish a long-lasting career. She not only maintained her relevance but also established a new benchmark for pop music by embracing change and taking artistic chances.

In retrospect, *Future Nostalgia* was evidently more than a single record. It was a declaration. It demonstrated Dua Lipa's willingness to take the lead, try new things, and develop. When she truly realized her potential as an artist, it was a pivotal moment. And she kept the same daring attitude as she went on, growing her impact in activism, fashion, and other fields.

Future Nostalgia demonstrated that Dua Lipa was not merely copying other artists,

Dua Lipa

even though her journey was far from complete. She was making her own.

Chapter 5: Fashion Forward – Redefining Pop Culture

In addition to being a music phenomenon, Dua Lipa is a fashion trendsetter. She has become one of the most significant people in pop culture throughout the years thanks to her daring fashion sense, unafraid decisions, and constantly changing persona. Similar to her music, her fashion choices challenge conventions, push boundaries and create new trends that both designers and fans admire. Unquestionably, Dua has influenced fashion and redefined what it means to be a contemporary pop artist by using her platform. Together, they have established a distinctive and identifiable brand, and her image is as compelling as her music.

Dua Lipa

Dua was aware of the power of clothes from the start of her career. She knew that style was more than simply clothes; it was a declaration, a manifestation of her creativity, and a means of expressing her identity. Dua wasn't scared to stand apart, unlike many other artists who were content to follow trends. She blended modern aesthetics with aspects of vintage design, fusing luxury couture with streetwear in novel and intriguing ways. Leading fashion designers adored her for her ability to effortlessly combine many styles, viewing her as the ideal inspiration for their creations.

Her ascent to fame on the red carpet was one of the turning points in her fashion career. She tried a variety of appearances when she first started in the business, but as her confidence grew, she created a

Dua Lipa

distinctive image that was edgy and glamorous. Whether it was futuristic metallic skirts, vintage-inspired corsets, or giant jackets in vibrant colors, Dua made sure every presentation was one to remember. Fans and fashion critics immediately recognized her willingness to take chances, and she soon rose to prominence as one of the most-watched celebrities at important events.

A significant turning point in her fashion career was her collaboration with Versace. What many followers already knew—that she was a contemporary symbol who personified strength, independence, and individuality—was recognized by the high-end design house. Versace's famously striking designs, vivid hues, and strong forms were a wonderful fit for Dua's style.

Dua Lipa

She was chosen to represent the brand in 2021, and her gorgeous appearances that combined traditional elegance with modern edge dazzled the world. She later walked the Versace catwalk, which is uncommon for a musician, demonstrating that her impact went beyond simply dressing in high-end clothing and that she was now a part of the fashion industry.

Dua worked with many other designers and companies in addition to Versace. She collaborated with brands like Valentino, Mugler, Balenciaga, and Yves Saint Laurent, frequently being among the first to don their most avant-garde designs. Fans immediately attempted to imitate her style, and her selections affected fashion trends all around the world. Her attire, which included everything from classic neon

Dua Lipa

bodysuits to minidresses adorned with crystals, served as an inspiration to fashion enthusiasts worldwide. Dua actively shaped her appearance, collaborating closely with stylists and designers to make sure each ensemble reflected her individuality and creative vision, in contrast to many celebrities who depend on stylists to determine their image.

Her 2022 Grammy appearance was one of the most talked-about fashion events of her career. Dua showed up in a gorgeous early 1990s vintage Versace dress that supermodel Cindy Crawford had first worn. The garment, which had gold chain embellishments and a dramatic black leather design, represented her ties to both contemporary and historical fashion luminaries. Her ability to give an old-school

Dua Lipa

style a contemporary, strong vibe was hailed by both fans and reviewers. This instance demonstrated that Dua was creating trends rather than merely following them, fusing the past and the future in a manner that only genuine style icons could.

Her impact extended beyond runway performances and red carpets. In addition, Dua expresses herself through her dress in her music videos, live appearances, and street style. She adopted a futuristic disco style in her hit song "Levitating," donning dazzling 1970s-inspired attire with contemporary touches. Her use of vivid hues, metallics, and whimsical silhouettes during her "Future Nostalgia" period was a wonderful fit for the retro-futuristic tone of the record. She demonstrated that her images were as powerful as her voice by

Dua Lipa

turning every music video and converting it into a fashion statement.

Dua has a significant influence on streetwear and high fashion. She made informal fashion equally significant, in contrast to many celebrities who only wore fancy clothes to events. She sparked a new trend of carefree yet fashionable style, whether she was seen sporting spectacular jackets with striking accessories, loose denim with crop tops, or oversized blazers with shoes. Her everyday clothes were enthusiastically followed by fans, demonstrating that her effect on fashion was not just in the upscale realm of haute couture but also in actual wardrobes all over the world.

The relationship between dua and fashion was about empowerment rather than

Dua Lipa

just personal taste.She frequently discussed how clothes may give one a sense of strength and self-assurance. In interviews, she talked about how embracing her uniqueness through dress experimentation inspired her admirers to follow suit. She broke conventional beauty standards and promoted diversity and body acceptance by dressing in ways that embraced a variety of body forms. Her self-assurance encouraged many young people to express themselves without fear, demonstrating that fashion was about identity and self-love as much as looks.

She was a cultural force because of her ability to effortlessly combine fashion and music. Her style changed along with her music. She was renowned for her edgy streetwear looks when she first started

Dua Lipa

out in the business, but as she developed as an artist, her taste in clothing got more sophisticated, avant-garde, and high-end. Her musical development from a young star to a worldwide icon was reflected in this transition. She kept her audience interested and involved by reinventing her style with every album, just as she did with herself.

She furthered her fashion influence in 2023 by collaborating with a prominent company to launch her own collection. Her distinctive style—bold, lively, and unabashedly stylish—was represented in this collection. Dua's collection perfectly captured her personality, in contrast to many celebrity fashion lines that seemed divorced from their individuality. It was an additional step in establishing her as a creative force

Dua Lipa

influencing the fashion industry in addition to being a fashion icon.

Style is more than just dressing well, as demonstrated by Dua Lipa's fashion journey. It's also about encouraging people, embracing originality, and making a statement. She has demonstrated the connection between fashion and music and how each influences an artist's identity. She stands out from many of her colleagues due to her daring approach to both, making her a genuine pop culture pioneer.

Her influence on the fashion industry will undoubtedly only increase as she develops more. Whether performing live, on the red carpet, or in daily life, Dua Lipa continues to be a potent illustration of how fashion can be a vehicle for cultural influence and self-expression. She is a

Dua Lipa

celebrity who defines the present and influences the future because of her ability to combine the past and present, as well as tradition and innovation.

Dua Lipa

Chapter 6: Breaking Barriers – Cultural Impact and Diversity

Pop diva Dua Lipa is not all that she is. She is a force that keeps shattering barriers in the music industry, a voice for diversity, and a symbol of change. She has been a standout from the start of her career, not just because of her strong voice and memorable songs but also because she speaks up for frequently ignored people, challenges industry norms, and reflects her background. Her accomplishment goes beyond music; it's about demonstrating to the world that talent knows no bounds and that diversity strengthens the industry.

Her upbringing has greatly influenced Dua Lipa's work and the principles she uphold. She was raised profoundly aware of what it

Dua Lipa

meant to be different because her parents were Albanian immigrants from Kosovo. She was reared in London, a city renowned for its multiculturalism after her parents fled their country before she was born in pursuit of better prospects. She gained a broader view of the world as a result, but she also became more conscious of the difficulties faced by many minorities and immigrants. When she returned to Kosovo as a teenager, she saw how hard life could be for people in a war-torn nation. She incorporated these experiences into her singing career, giving her a strong sense of identity and purpose.

From the first day she entered the music business, Dua defied convention. Many female artists anticipated a specific image— soft, polished, and simple to market—but

Dua Lipa

Dua, however, was unique. In contrast to the high-pitched vocals in vogue at the time, she had a deep, velvety voice. She didn't hesitate to combine high fashion with streetwear in daring, unorthodox ways. People soon started to notice her because of her self-assurance and refusal to fit in.

One of the most significant ways Dua Lipa has broken down barriers is by promoting cultural diversity in her music. In contrast to many prominent musicians who only use one style, she has embraced a variety of global influences. She has collaborated with musicians from various backgrounds, incorporating pop, dance, and even Middle Eastern and Latin rhythms into her compositions. This has enabled her to reach a worldwide audience, demonstrating that

Dua Lipa

language and nationality shouldn't be barriers to music's universal appeal.

Dua has spoken out on significant causes using her platform in addition to her songs. She has never shied away from discussing her background and the challenges of coming from an immigrant household. In interviews, she talked about how her parents' perseverance motivated her and how they had to work hard to provide her with a better life. She has also tried to increase awareness of the dilemma affecting those who are compelled to flee their countries because of war or economic hardship and has been outspoken about the difficulties experienced by refugees.

Dua's performances and music videos demonstrate her dedication to diversity. Incorporating dancers, models, and

Dua Lipa

creatives from all backgrounds into her work has always been a priority for her. She has demonstrated that representation is important by performing with musicians from many cultures and by including varied groups of people in her videos. She performed a dance routine with people of many ethnicities, body shapes, and gender identities at an awards event, which was one of her most impactful performances. It made a powerful statement: everyone should be acknowledged and honored.

Dua Lipa has had a big influence on the fashion industry in addition to music. She has stated that she creates her own trends, even if many celebrities follow them. She has collaborated with designers from throughout the globe, frequently showcasing companies that are founded by people of

Dua Lipa

color or that reflect her heritage. Her selections demonstrate that everyone should have a voice in fashion, just as in music.

She also has an impact on activism. She has been a vocal advocate for mental health awareness, LGBTQ+ rights, and gender equality. She has advocated for groups that want to make the world more inclusive and spoken out against discrimination on social media. She established the Sunny Hill Foundation in 2022, which is named after the Kosovo neighborhood where her family is from. The charity provides educational and artistic possibilities to young people in Kosovo.It demonstrated that success should be utilized to uplift others and was her way of giving back to the community that had shaped her.

Dua Lipa

Dua has also not hesitated to expose the shortcomings of the music industry. She has discussed how female artists are expected to continuously prove themselves and are frequently subjected to harsh criticism than their male peers. By moving forward and refusing to let other people's expectations define her, she has fought against these unfair standards. She demonstrated that talent should be acknowledged without regard to gender when she stated in an interview that she didn't want to be merely a "female artist," but rather just an artist.

Dua has had numerous instances throughout her career that demonstrated she was more than just a pop star—rather, she was a societal force. Her Grammy win for Best New Artist was one such instance.

Dua Lipa

"I guess this year, we really stepped up," she said as she accepted the prize on stage, a statement that struck a chord with many. It was in response to a statement made by a music executive earlier that year that said female musicians needed to "step up" in order to be successful. They already had, as evidenced by her victory.

Her performance at the Brit Awards, where she honored frontline workers during the COVID-19 outbreak, was another pivotal event. She called for improved wages and working conditions for critical workers while wearing a costume influenced by British working-class culture. It served as a reminder that music can be a potent force for change in addition to being a kind of entertainment.

Dua Lipa

Dua's influence extends beyond her professional life. She has demonstrated that success is achievable regardless of one's background by providing opportunities for artists from a variety of backgrounds. She has encouraged a new generation of musicians to accept their own identities and use music to share their stories by remaining loyal to herself.

The main lesson to be learned from Dua Lipa's journey is that long-lasting societal transformation results from accepting diversity and questioning conventions. She has demonstrated how art, fashion, and music ought to represent the diverse world we live in, which is full with voices, tales, and viewpoints. Her accomplishments demonstrate that being unique is an asset rather than a drawback.

Dua Lipa

It's evident from examining her early influences that Dua's experiences influenced her distinct identity. She had a profound grasp of what it meant to break down barriers as a result of her cosmopolitan upbringing, international moves, and watching her parents start over. She gained the courage to pursue a field that frequently attempts to categorize people—and to defy classification—thanks to these encounters.

Her influence is growing along with her profession. She is raising the bar for what it means to be a modern artist with every new album, project, and partnership. She is influencing the culture around her in addition to creating music, demonstrating that diversity is something to be lived rather than merely discussed.

Dua Lipa

One thing is certain: Dua Lipa is more than just a music sensation, even though her narrative is far from over. She is a movement, a representation of transformation, and a reminder that you have the power to alter the world when you accept who you are.

Dua Lipa

Chapter 7: Accolades and Recognition –
The Awards Journey

Dua Lipa's musical career has been nothing short of remarkable. From a little kid sharing song covers on YouTube to a worldwide pop sensation, she has put in countless hours to create a career that has changed the music industry and delighted millions of people. Although skill and diligence are important, industry recognition provides additional legitimacy. Dua has won some of the most prominent music accolades throughout the years, demonstrating that her colleagues and industry professionals respect her work and that she is well-liked. These honors testify to her impact, inventiveness, and capacity for global connection.

Dua Lipa

Dua made her breakthrough by releasing her debut album of the same name. Her rich, distinctive voice and talent for writing catchy yet meaningful words were fully displayed in the album's numerous popular tracks. Songs like "IDGAF" and "New Rules" became anthems for empowerment and self-assurance. The album's popularity resulted in multiple nominations for awards. Dua won British Breakthrough Act and Best British Female Solo Artist at the 2018 Brit Awards. Her position in the music industry was cemented at that moment. As she stood on that podium, receiving her first significant honor, she couldn't help but think back on the years of arduous effort, rejection, and tenacity that had led her to this point.

Dua Lipa

The Grammy Awards are the highest honor in music, even though the Brit Awards were a huge accomplishment. Most artists dream of winning a Grammy, and Dua was no different.She was nominated for Best Dance Recording and Best New Artist in 2019. She was overcome with emotion when her name was shouted for Best New Artist, even though the competition was fierce. She expressed her gratitude for the chance to compose music and the significance of artists remaining loyal to themselves in her acceptance speech. Her career took a significant turn after receiving this honor, demonstrating that she was not only a rising star but also a powerful player in the field.

The duo didn't end there. She achieved unprecedented popularity with the publication of Future Nostalgia, her second

Dua Lipa

album. With its catchy sounds and stirring lyrics, the CD was a celebration of dance-pop music. Given that many musicians at the time were moving toward slower, more emotive tracks, it was a daring decision. But Dua had faith in her idea, and it worked. The album achieved global success, reaching the top of the charts and receiving praise from critics.

After the industry took notice, nominations for awards began to flood in. Dua received nominations in multiple key categories, including Album of the Year, at the 2021 Grammy Awards. She joined some of the greatest pop musicians of all time when she won Best Pop Vocal Album, an amazing accomplishment. This victory was particularly noteworthy since it demonstrated that she was more than a one-hit wonder. She had developed as an artist, demonstrating that skill, diligence, and a strong sense of self were the foundations of her success.

The influence Dua has on music was still acknowledged by the Brit Awards. She won British Female Solo Artist and British Album of the Year in 2021. She dedicated her victory to frontline workers who had assisted people during the COVID-19 outbreak in a moving acceptance speech. She was obviously aware of the influence her platform had and wanted to use it to raise awareness of worthy issues.

Dua has received recognition at various significant award shows in addition to the Grammy and Brit Awards. Her numerous MTV Europe Music Awards demonstrate her significant global influence. Additionally,

Dua Lipa

she has won the American Music Awards, demonstrating her widespread appeal in the US. She has even received recognition from the Billboard Music Awards, which are determined by chart performance, demonstrating that she is not only a darling among critics but also a commercial success.

Dua's performance at the 2021 Grammy Awards stands out as one of the most memorable events in her award journey. She showcased her dancing abilities and stage presence while performing a mix of her greatest hits while wearing a stunning pink costume. It was a turning point that demonstrated she was a complete performer and not just a singer. Social media erupted in applause as the audience was enthralled. These kinds of moments

Dua Lipa

serve as a reminder to the public of why she is among the most fascinating musicians working today.

Winning honors is about more than simply the trophies; it's about what they stand for. Each honor serves as evidence of Dua's progress. Many questioned her when she first started. She was advised that she didn't fit the usual pop star mold and that her voice was too deep. However, she was unwilling to alter her identity. Rather, she stood out by utilizing her peculiarities. Now that she has won numerous accolades and gained notoriety across the globe, she has demonstrated that the greatest way to succeed is to remain true to yourself.

Every prize has a backstory. Exciting acceptance speeches and glitzy red carpets are only the tip of the iceberg. Dua has

Dua Lipa

encountered difficulties behind the scenes, including as self-doubt and rigorous rehearsals. There have been times when she has doubted her abilities and abilities. Nevertheless, she persisted each time, confident that her passion for music would overcome any challenge.

Achieving success is never simple, and honors are not given out at random. Dua's perseverance, enthusiasm, and capacity to engage audiences through her songs are the reasons behind her industry fame. Every honor serves as a reminder that perseverance pays off and that with enough effort, aspirations can come true.

Her influence only grows as she develops as an artist. Winning accolades is a privilege, but her influence on her fans and the music business is what counts most.

Dua Lipa

She has raised the bar for pop music by fusing classic elements with contemporary ideas. What really sets her apart is her ability to write songs that inspire joy, empowerment, and understanding in listeners.

Dua's quest for accolades is far from finished. She pushes limits and reimagines what it means to be a pop star with each record. She has a great future ahead of her, and she will undoubtedly receive more recognition. One thing, though, never changes regardless of how many awards she receives: her passion for music and her dedication to writing songs that uplift others.

She has been able to work with some of the greatest names in the industry because to her notoriety on international stages.Her

Dua Lipa

influence will only grow as she continues to create music because of her ability to collaborate with musicians from many backgrounds and genres. In addition to securing additional accolades, the next phase of her career will focus on solidifying her reputation as one of the most significant artists of her generation.

The honors and acclaim Dua Lipa has received are a testament to her tenacity, fervor, and strength of self-belief. They demonstrate that she is a distinguishing voice in contemporary music rather than merely a passing celebrity. And as she develops further, she will continue to motivate the upcoming generation of musicians by demonstrating that anything is achievable with perseverance and sincerity.

Dua Lipa

Chapter 8: Global Phenomenon – Collaborations and International Success

It took Dua Lipa some time to become a worldwide superstar. She put in a lot of effort to have her voice heard, and it paid off in ways she never could have predicted. Her capacity to connect with audiences everywhere propelled her ascent to stardom, from playing in little places to selling out enormous global arenas. Her smart partnerships with international artists were a major factor in her success. She broadened her audience and presented her music to listeners worldwide by collaborating with musicians from many genres and cultures.

Dua already had a significant following in the UK and Europe in the early years of her

Dua Lipa

career, but she desired more. Her goal was to create music that would be enjoyed worldwide. She was aware that to achieve that, she would need to work with artists who could introduce her to new audiences and venture beyond her comfort zone. She collaborated with Sean Paul on the song "No Lie," her first significant international project. The song included a groove with a Caribbean feel, and Dua's strong vocals blended flawlessly with Sean Paul's distinctive style. The song's international success demonstrated her potential as more than simply a UK pop sensation.

Her partnerships expanded along with her career. The song "One Kiss," which she co-wrote with Calvin Harris, became a huge summer hit and one of the year's biggest singles, topping charts in multiple countries.
Dua Lipa

For Dua, this was a pivotal moment. It demonstrated that she was here to stay and wasn't just a one-hit wonder. She began to receive more requests for collaborations from artists all around the world.

Her next significant partnership was on the song "One Day," which she co-produced with French producer DJ Snake and Spanish singer J Balvin. This song appealed to listeners from various cultural backgrounds since it combined pop, electronic, and Latin music. She was introduced to fans of Latin music via the song, particularly in nations like Brazil, Spain, and Mexico. Her music transcended linguistic boundaries thanks to collaborations with musicians from various backgrounds. People could relate to her

Dua Lipa

energy and sense the emotions in her voice even if they didn't comprehend the lyrics.

Her partnership with K-pop sensations BTS was one of her most fruitful partnerships. BTS members were featured in the song "Dream Glow," which fused K-pop and Western pop elements. Because of BTS's enormous global fan base, particularly in Asia and the US, this partnership was noteworthy. Collaborating with them enabled Dua Lipa to connect with millions of new listeners who might not have otherwise heard her music. She was now acknowledged as a truly international performer who could engage audiences from a wide range of backgrounds and cultures.

However, she became a global celebrity for reasons other than her partnerships. Her fan

Dua Lipa

base grew significantly as a result of her international tours. She went on her first international tour following the success of her debut album. She performed in front of thousands of admirers who were familiar with every word of her songs while touring Europe, North America, Asia, and South America. For her, it was a moving experience to watch people from other nations join in on her songs. It demonstrated to her that music was a common language that united people from all walks of life.

Her tours were experiences rather than merely performances. She worked very hard to make every performance unique. She aimed to give her followers the impression that they were a part of something extraordinary through breathtaking scenery and exuberant performances. She also took

Dua Lipa

care to incorporate aspects of the local culture from the locations she visited. She danced to native music while she was in Brazil. She honored Japanese customs when she was there. Fans felt even closer to her as a result of this. She was embracing their culture in addition to performing in their nation.

Her performance at the Grammy Awards was another noteworthy event in her narrative of worldwide achievement. One of the greatest accolades an artist can receive is a Grammy, and Dua Lipa not only took home the trophy but also dazzled the crowd with an amazing performance. She performed with St. Vincent, fusing their styles in a way that demonstrated her range as a performer. People all throughout the world saw her that night as an artist with

Dua Lipa

genuine talent and passion, not just a pop celebrity.

Her influence on international media was equally as potent as her musical output. She gained popularity as a talk show guest, captivating viewers with her humor and grounded demeanor. She also appeared in prominent magazines like Elle, Rolling Stone, and Vogue, demonstrating her status as a fashion star in addition to being a gifted performer. She became a fashion industry trendsetter, and designers from all over the world wanted her to wear their creations.

Dua Lipa's streaming figures also demonstrated her widespread fame. Her tracks dominated music services like Apple Music and Spotify. Every month, millions of listeners tuned in, making her one of the most streamed female musicians. The fact

Dua Lipa

that she was able to sustain her accomplishment added to its impressiveness. Dua has a career where every album and single she released became a worldwide smash when many musicians only have one or two hit songs.

She never lost sight of her roots, even with her hectic schedule. She frequently discussed her origins and the significance of representing her ancestry. By using her platform, she raised awareness of problems impacting Kosovo and other regions of the world. As a result, she gained even more respect, both as a performer and as someone who was concerned about changing the world.

Meeting a fan in Japan who had picked up English simply by listening to her songs stands out as one of the most memorable

Dua Lipa

moments of her international tour. The fan informed her that her music had transformed their lives and motivated them to learn the language. She was reminded of why she enjoyed creating music by moments like these. Touching people's hearts and having a genuine influence on their lives was more important than celebrity or accolades.

With perseverance, hard work, and the correct approach, Dua Lipa's path from a little kid uploading covers on YouTube to a worldwide pop sensation is evidence that dreams may come true. In order to reach a wider audience and ensure that her music spoke to people from all cultural backgrounds, she engaged in international partnerships. She was able to build strong relationships with her followers during her

Dua Lipa

international tours, demonstrating to them her genuine concern for their support. She also demonstrated through her media presence that she was a worldwide icon in addition to being a vocalist.

A key lesson from her tale is that international exposure is more than just celebrity. It's about developing yourself, discovering new cultures, and showcasing your art to the world. Dua Lipa took advantage of every chance to work together, perform, and meet new people. She didn't confine herself to a single genre, nation, or style of thought. Rather, she gave herself permission to change, to take chances, and to continue pushing the envelope of what was conceivable.

It's amazing to see how far she's gone when comparing her early career. She first gained

Dua Lipa

notoriety online for her innovations in digital technology. She didn't stop there, though. She went beyond the internet, performing on stages across the globe and becoming well-known everywhere. Fans are excited to watch what she will accomplish next as she continues to develop.

The next phase of her life will center on something even more intimate—who she is outside of her celebrity. She has already established herself as a world-renowned figure. The world is now eager to discover more about the woman who created the music, her hardships, and the lessons she has discovered. The best may still be in store for her; her journey is far from complete.

Dua Lipa

Chapter 9: Personal Growth – Challenges and Triumphs

It took more than great songs, glitzy red carpets, or stylish moments for Dua Lipa to become a worldwide pop sensation. A young woman dealing with personal difficulties, self-doubt, and stressful situations was hidden behind the spotlight. For her, personal growth was a process of learning, falling, rising, and changing rather than something that just happened. She had many highs and lows on her path to success, and each one helped to mold her into the person and artist she is today.

Dua Lipa had to work to establish herself right from the start. Her upbringing in a musically inclined family gave her a feeling of purpose, but success was not always simple. At the age of fifteen, returning to London alone was both a thrilling and terrifying experience. In times of uncertainty, she had to continue to believe in herself, take care of herself, and perform side jobs to finance her dream. On certain days, she wondered if her dreams were too lofty or if she was good enough. However, she resisted allowing fear to rule her.

When Dua first began posting covers to YouTube, she encountered doubt and rejection. Others informed her that her voice was too unusual or didn't appear proper. Because the music business is so competitive, not everyone thought she had what it required to succeed. However, she remained loyal to her sound rather than altering herself to suit people's desires. Instead of trying to sound like everyone

Dua Lipa

else, she embraced her distinctive voice, which was deep and velvety.

The difficulties persisted even after she signed a record deal. There was a new pressure that came with being in the spotlight. Everyone had an opinion on everything, including her life, fashion choices, and music. She needed to develop the ability to take criticism without allowing it to undermine her self-esteem. Everything has become even more acute because of social media. Although it was a tool that aided in her discovery, it also turned into a venue for the rapid spread of negativity. She had to contend with rumors, hateful remarks, and irrational expectations all the time.

Her mental health significantly impacted her trip. Dua Lipa experienced periods of stress

Dua Lipa

and self-doubt, like many other artists. The pressure to remain at the top, to always release hit songs, and to always be flawless was unbearable. She has been forthright about the reality that fame does not exempt one from hardships. She wondered if she could manage everything that came with success at times when she felt exhausted. Whether that meant taking breaks, spending time with loved ones, or just letting herself feel emotions without fear, she needed to figure out how to take care of herself.

The publication of Dua's second album, *Future Nostalgia*, was one of the most pivotal events in her career. Although it was a great success, the stress and uncertainty behind the scenes were not visible to the public. She needed to demonstrate that she wasn't a one-hit wonder. She aimed to make

Dua Lipa

an album that stretched the limits of pop music and accurately reflected who she was. The CD came to represent her development as a person and a musician. Things demonstrated her self-assurance, risk-taking skills, and refusal to play things safe.

Even with all of her accomplishments, Dua still has difficulties. Finding a balance between her personal and professional lives has been one of the most difficult challenges. Being famous may be isolating. Maintaining intimate relationships can be challenging when you're constantly on the road, performing and working on new projects. Despite how hectic life can get, she has talked about how crucial it is to maintain relationships with friends and family. She tries to protect the relationships

Dua Lipa

that are most important to her and to keep her personal life private.

Learning to speak up for what's important to her has been a significant aspect of her personal development. She became aware that she had a platform to voice her opinions on significant matters as her popularity grew. She has steadfastly supported refugee assistance, mental health awareness, and women's rights. Her own family's history of fleeing Kosovo and establishing a new life in London is the source of her involvement. She wants to utilize her achievements to encourage people to fight for a better future because she knows what it means to do so.

Dua's journey has been one of embracing vulnerability. She is aware that fans find her more accessible when she displays her true,

Dua Lipa

flawed self. She doesn't act differently from who she is. She has discovered that acknowledging one's weaknesses and strengths is the key to having true confidence. Even in the face of adversity, she inspires people to believe in themselves.Her message is straightforward: success does not need perfection. All you need to do is keep moving forward, keep learning, and never lose faith in yourself.

In retrospect, each hardship Dua Lipa encountered helped to mold her. She learned a lot from the challenges of being a teenager in a new place, the necessity to stay true to herself, the mental toll of celebrity, and the pressure to succeed in the music business. They strengthened her will, increased her resolve,

Dua Lipa

and strengthened her bond with the person she aspires to be.

As she develops, she never loses sight of what really counts: creating inspirational music, upholding her moral principles, and utilizing her voice to change the world. Achieving a final goal is not the goal of personal growth. It is about continuously improving, learning, and changing. Every obstacle is merely a new chapter in Dua Lipa's path, and she is prepared to take on whatever is ahead with courage, passion, and a fearless heart.

Dua Lipa

Chapter 10: The Future of Pop – Enduring Legacy and Vision Ahead

Dua Lipa's transformation from an aspirational young girl with a dream to a worldwide superstar has already profoundly impacted the music industry. What happens next, though? Few artists ever can shape the future as she is, and her impact on pop music, fashion, and culture continues to expand. The industry around her is changing along with her. Many musicians in today's pop scene are influenced by her distinct sound, audacious self-assurance, and ability to combine various influences to create something novel and captivating. Dua Lipa has established a foundation that guarantees her continued prominence in pop music for years, in contrast to many other musicians who come and go.

Her avant-garde approach to music revolutionized the composition and consumption of mainstream tunes. When she started working in the field, slow, melancholic songs controlled much of mainstream music. Dua contributed to reviving lively, danceable pop music with catchy songs and energizing sounds. Songs like "Levitating" and "Don't Start Now" demonstrated that people still enjoyed music that got them moving. This change impacts a new generation of musicians who are now adopting Dua's disco-inspired beats, throwback sounds, and empowering lyrics.

Dua Lipa is shaping pop music's future, according to industry experts. Music

Dua Lipa

producers and reviewers have lauded her ability to take traditional elements and make them feel contemporary. She doesn't hesitate to take chances, whether working with surprising partners or fusing pop and house music. As a result, her music strikes a balance that few musicians can accomplish: it seems both new and familiar. She is probably going to continue pushing the envelope as she experiments more, creating new looks and trends.

Dua's influence goes beyond music to include pop culture and fashion. She has collaborated with leading designers, produced distinctive styles that impact millions of people, and contributed to redefining what it means to be a contemporary pop star. Dua constantly reinvents herself, in contrast to many

Dua Lipa

musicians who only work in one style, demonstrating that pop music is about more than just sound; it's also about personality, self-assurance, and visual storytelling. The next generation of musicians will probably go this route since they realize that, in the modern world, being a musician also entails setting cultural trends and becoming a fashion star.

Looking ahead, there are countless opportunities for Dua Lipa. Her next moves are the subject of much conjecture among fans and industry insiders. Others think that, like previous musicians who have made a successful move into movies, she may embark on more acting parts. Some predict that she will keep growing her fashion influence and perhaps start her company. She also has a good chance of launching

Dua Lipa

her record company, where she will use her background to coach and support upcoming artists. One thing is for sure: she will approach anything she decides to accomplish with the same fervor and commitment that initially made her a household name.

Dua Lipa's capacity to foresee and welcome the future is among her most fascinating qualities. She has an innate sense of what will happen next when other artists find it difficult to stay up to date with evolving trends. This was demonstrated by her album *Future Nostalgia*, in which she established a sound that was both future and timeless, paving the way for the next phase of pop music. Whatever she does next will probably determine the next

Dua Lipa

chapter of pop culture because of her ability to remain ahead of the curve.

Already, her legacy is beginning to take shape. She is frequently cited as an influence by aspiring artists. Many respect her for being true to herself while still developing and changing. Dua has always been genuine, which is a major factor in why fans relate to her, in contrast to certain celebrities who alter their appearance to blend in. More and more musicians will look to her as a model for success while adhering to their artistic vision as pop music develops.

Dua's impact extends beyond design and music as well. She has advocated for women's rights, mental health, and refugee assistance, among other significant global concerns, using her position. Being from an

Dua Lipa

immigrant family, she is aware of the difficulties that many people encounter, and she has never shied away from using her voice for the greater good. She might become even more active in the future and utilize her notoriety to advocate for causes that are important to her.

Some people envision her directing music festivals that showcase female performers, coaching up-and-coming musicians, or even starting a company that assists aspiring musicians in breaking into the business. According to others, she will keep reinventing live performances by utilizing technology to produce immersive musical experiences that surpass what audiences have ever witnessed. Many of the concepts she helped pioneer will probably be incorporated into pop music in the future.

Dua Lipa

It's evident from looking back at her path that Dua Lipa's tale is one of ardor, tenacity, and unafraid inventiveness. She has demonstrated that with perseverance and hard effort, dreams can come true, going from a small girl singing in her bedroom to a global sensation. She started trends rather than merely following them. She altered how people view pop culture in addition to creating music. Her experience serves as a reminder that vision, self-assurance, and a willingness to take chances are just as important for success as skill.

Pop music is constantly changing, yet some performers make an impression that never goes away. One of such artists is Dua Lipa. She has already made history, regardless of where her journey takes her next. And the road she cleared will continue to inspire

Dua Lipa

upcoming generations of artists. Pop has a bright future, and Dua Lipa will always be a part of it.

Made in United States
Cleveland, OH
08 April 2025